Bridgetender's Boy

by Linda J. Barth

illustrated by Doreen Lorenzetti

Published by Canal History and Technology Press

National Canal Museum

30 Centre Square, Easton, Pennsylvania 18042

This story takes place in 1868 along the Delaware and Raritan Canal in New Jersey. On this canal, all of the bridges swung to the side to allow boats to pass. Even very tall vessels could use the canal because there were no overhead obstructions.

Ten-year-old Josh Riley lives in the village of Griggstown. He is the son of the bridgetender, who pushes the bridge to the side when boats come through. Every day Josh sees boats that come from faraway places. He wishes that someday he, too, could travel to big cities and see the world.

DEDICATION

To Bob, my favorite proofreader and the love of my life – LJB

To my dear friends and family, especially John, Christopher, Jonathan and Cheyanna, with love and thanks – DLH

Special thanks to Gary Kleinedler for his wonderful map-making skills.

ISBN 0-930973-34-8 soft cover

ISBN 0-930973-35-6 hard cover

Library of Congress Control Number: 2004116036

**Canal History and
Technology Press**

National Canal Museum
30 Centre Square, Easton, PA 18042-7743

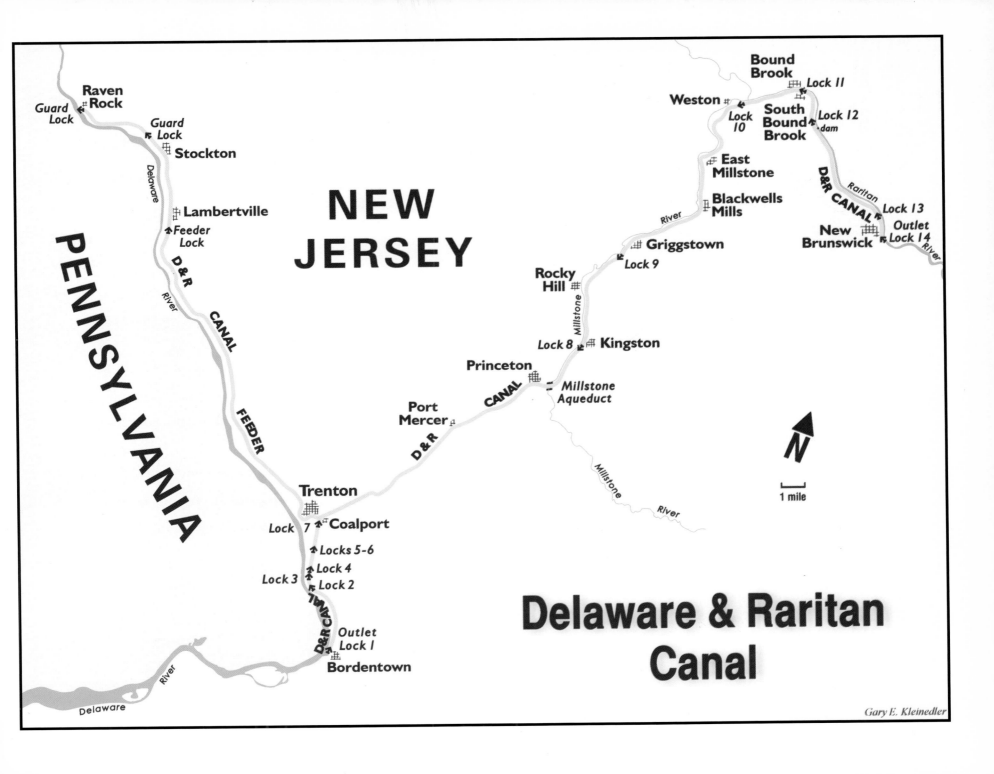

Delaware & Raritan Canal

"*Woo-o-o-o!*" The low moan of the conch shell floated across the still water of the canal. Josh Riley listened as he worked his knife, carefully peeling away bits of wood. Slowly, a shape began to appear — feathers, delicately formed, and a head with a beak. He sat back and admired his work. The eagle carving looked almost real, as if it could fly away at any moment.

Josh looked around at his little village with just a few homes and one store. If only *he* could fly away like his eagle and see the world beyond Griggstown. He would soar over the canal and follow it to the towns and cities along the waterway. He might even fly farther, and see the oceans and mountains and deserts he had only read about. But those dreams would have to wait.

"Joshua! Boat coming!" shouted his sister Sarah impatiently. "Leave your whittling and come swing the bridge!"

Reluctantly, Josh laid down his knife and left his workbench. He didn't mind helping his father, but he wished he didn't have to stay here each and every day, opening and closing the "A" frame swing bridge. Heading for the bridge, he paused to look upcanal. The approaching canalboat was the *Atlantic*. The captain was Jeremiah Van Doren, a tall, muscular man whom Josh and Sarah had known since they were babies.

The Van Doren family traveled together every day, Josh thought. Their boat was their house. They lived aboard and moved from place to place. The Van Dorens carried coal and farm products up and down the canal, all the way across New Jersey.

"I'd like to do that, instead of being stuck here in this little town, sunup to sundown, every day. I'd like to see the rest of the world. Big cities, like New Brunswick and Trenton, with their busy docks. Packet boats that took people to New York and Philadelphia. And fast trains that crossed the state. New people, new places. If only . . . "

Josh spotted his friend, young Sam Van Doren, leading the mules along the towpath, so he hurried to the bridge and pushed it to the side. The bridge came to a stop along the bank opposite the towpath, leaving a narrow channel for the boat to pass through.

Ten-year-old Josh did most of the work of swinging the "A" frame bridge when his father was away from home. His little sister often hopped on for the ride. Tending the bridge here at Griggstown was easy, because it was so well balanced. Even Josh, who wasn't too strong, could swing it with no trouble. His father Michael worked hard to keep the gears and wheels of the bridge in good working order.

Josh and Sam exchanged greetings across the canal as the young mule driver walked by with Dorrie and Daisy, the Jersey team that pulled the canalboat along the Delaware and Raritan Canal. Josh could never figure out why a pair of mules, one brown and one white, was called a Jersey team. Maybe Sam could tell him.

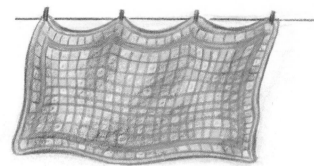

The *Atlantic* maneuvered through the narrow channel next to the bridge. Sarah called a greeting to Sam's sister Molly, who stood next to her father at the tiller.

At that moment, a rabbit skittered across the towpath, spooking Daisy, the lead mule. Daisy reared up, knocking Sam down and kicking his leg. He grasped his leg in pain and, off balance, fell headlong onto the ground. His forehead smacked the hard earth of the towpath, knocking him out, and he slowly rolled into the canal. With hardly a splash, he disappeared under the muddy water.

Immediately his father ran to the bow, leaped off the boat, and jumped into the canal. Josh, seeing his friend in trouble, quickly closed the bridge and raced across to the towpath. He waited nervously, trying to see through the murky, brown water. Finally, the captain's head popped up above the surface, his strong arms around Sam's chest.

Josh helped drag Sam up the steep bank. Mrs. Van Doren had steered the boat to the bank and jumped ashore. She spoke softly to her son as her husband carried Sam to a grassy spot beside the towpath.

Captain Van Doren lifted Sam and held him upside to get the water out of his lungs. To everyone's relief, Sam began gasping and coughing. As his breathing slowly returned to normal, the young mule driver opened his eyes and reached up to touch the baseball-sized lump on the side of his head. He grimaced as his father examined his bleeding leg.

"Daisy must have kicked you," the Captain said. "You may have a broken leg."

Relieved that Sam was awake, Josh ran down the towpath to stop the mules.

Timidly approaching Dorrie and Daisy, he spoke gently at first. "Easy, girls. It's all right. You just calm down."

As the mules slowed, they seemed to tower above Josh. But he took a deep breath and stopped them with a sharp, "Whoa!"

Captain Van Doren called, "Josh, get a board so we can carry Sam to the house!" Josh raced to the woodshed and hurried back with a wide plank. Together, they gently rolled Sam onto the stretcher. As they carried him toward the bridgetender's house, Josh saw his parents' wagon coming down the road.

"Mom! Dad! Sam's been hurt! His leg may be broken."

"We'll telegraph for Doc Wilson," Mr. Riley said.

"Sam should wait here until the doctor comes," said Mrs. Riley. "Why doesn't he just stay here with us 'til he's able to walk?"

"That's too much to ask of you, Sally!" said Mrs. Van Doren. "You have enough to do taking care of your *own* family."

"Not at all! You just leave him here with us while you finish your trip. It'll be no trouble and he can sleep in the parlor."

"We'd hate to trouble you, but it would be a blessing. You know we have to get to New Brunswick with this load of coal, or we'll not be paid. But who can we get to drive the mules? Molly's too young and I've not been feelin' too well."

Josh looked hopefully at his father. This could be his chance to see the world outside of Griggstown! He *knew* he could learn to be a mule driver! Every day he watched the hoggees

who passed and he listened as they spoke to their animals. It might be scary, being alone on the towpath with those huge animals, but he just *knew* he could do it! As if reading his son's mind, Mr. Riley put his large hand on Josh's shoulder and said to the captain, "Would you be wantin' to teach Josh to drive the mules for you? We could spare him for a few weeks 'til Sam recovers."

And so it was decided. Josh grabbed an extra shirt and a pair of overalls, said good-bye to his family, crossed the bridge, and walked over to the mules on the towpath.

Mrs. Van Doren reminded Josh of the commands that Daisy and Dorrie already knew:

"Get up" — go.

"Whoa" — stop.

"Gee" — go to the right.

"Haw" — go to the left.

With a wave to his parents and a tentative "Get up" to the mules, Josh started out on the long walk to the end of the canal. Soon he passed a milepost that showed 20 miles to New Brunswick. Turning around, Josh could read on the backside, "24" — the number of miles in the other direction, to Bordentown, on the Delaware River. It seemed a long way, but he was sure he could do it.

In less than an hour, Captain Van Doren sounded the conch shell horn and soon the *Atlantic* passed through the bridge opening at Blackwells Mills.

"Good morning, Mr. Hopewell," bellowed the captain to the bridgetender.

"Hello to you, and who's your new mule driver?"

"I'm Josh Riley, the bridgetender's boy from Griggstown," Josh called over his shoulder as the boat floated through the opened bridge.

Not long after, they passed through the swing bridges at East Millstone and Weston. As they approached a lock, Captain Van Doren held the conch shell to his lips and blew again.

"I used to have a tin horn," he told Josh, "but I dropped it into the canal. Then I got this conch shell, cut off the end, and practiced blowing it." Josh heard the low, loud sound. He knew that the locktenders and bridgetenders could hear it a mile away, so they could get ready for the approaching boat. The captain made sure he blew a warning note, so he wouldn't be fined a day's pay.

As the *Atlantic* neared the lock, Josh saw the Millstone River on the other side of the towpath. Back home, the river was much farther away from the canal, but here it had meandered close, and met the Raritan River near Lock 10.

Captain Van Doren called to Josh, "When the mules reach the lock, stop them and take the line I throw to you. Loop

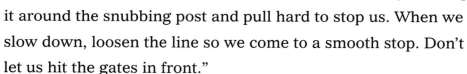

it around the snubbing post and pull hard to stop us. When we slow down, loosen the line so we come to a smooth stop. Don't let us hit the gates in front."

Josh followed the captain's orders and stopped the mules with a stern "Whoa!" With a little help from the locktender, he wrapped the line around the post and snubbed the boat to a stop. Daisy and Dorrie stood to the side of the lock, waiting patiently for the boat to lock down. The captain stepped off the boat, carrying two long, leather buckets filled with oats. Walking up to the animals, he carefully slipped the nosebags over the ears of each mule, so their faces could fit inside. Now Daisy and Dorrie could eat while they walked.

Josh watched as the locktender raised the heavy drop gate behind the boat and walked to the downstream end of the lock. Stepping out onto a narrow wooden plank attached to the massive gates, he used a lever to turn metal bars that were sticking up into the air. These bars were connected to small doors in the gates called wickets, far down under the water. The wickets opened and allowed the water to flow out of the lock chamber. As the water got lower, the boat went lower, too. Soon Josh saw that the roof of the vessel was below him, between the stone walls of the lock.

When enough water had flowed out, the water level inside the lock was even with the water on the downstream end, outside the lock. The locktender opened the gates. Captain Van Doren called to Josh to start the team moving, and the *Atlantic* was pulled smoothly out of the lock and on its way.

Now Josh saw the place where two mud-colored rivers met. The Millstone flowed into the Raritan, making one larger, wider river. Looking down, he realized that he was walking on a narrow strip of land, with the canal on one side and the swift-moving Raritan on the other, far below.

The conch horn sounded again, signaling their approach to Lock 11. Ahead, Josh saw the homes and stores in the little town of South Bound Brook. The village was tucked inside the curve of the canal, just like little Sarah being held in the curve of their mother's arm. Again Josh snubbed the boat to a stop, this time with no help, and watched the locktender open the wickets to let the water out. While Josh waited with the mules, Mrs. Van Doren handed him some bread and cheese for his lunch. The food helped him forget about his sore feet. He wasn't used to walking this far in one day. But he didn't mind having blisters on his feet if it meant leaving Griggstown and seeing so many new places.

Using the same procedure as before, the *Atlantic* locked down and continued downstream. Passing through the open bridge, Josh looked to his left and saw the hustle and bustle in Bound Brook, a larger town across the river. A long line of wagons waited until the boat passed and the bridgetender closed the span across the canal.

As the *Atlantic* sailed around South Bound Brook, the captain pointed out two sawmills and a boat yard. "We'll be stopping in town for supplies on our way back," he said. "But for now we have to get to New Brunswick as quickly as we can."

In no time at all, the *Atlantic* reached Lock 12 on the other side of town. Josh saw a dam across the Raritan River and asked Captain Van Doren about it. "That dam supplies water from the river to the canal," he answered. "It goes through an opening under the towpath. You can't see it from here. We'll be floating on Raritan River water from here to New Brunswick."

"Where does all the rest of the water come from?" Josh had often thought about that as he walked along. There wasn't enough rain to fill all these miles of canal.

"The water upstream of this dam comes all the way from the Delaware River, Josh," the captain explained. "A separate canal brings the water twenty-two miles downhill to meet this canal in Trenton. I'll show you if you're with us when we get there."

As they cruised the last five miles to New Brunswick, Josh wondered what he would see in the big city. He had heard the boatmen talk about the many factories, stores, docks, hotels, and boats there. "Will we have time to look around the city, Captain Van Doren?"

"I expect we can take a bit of a walk, my boy. I have to speak with Mr. Van Arsdalen at the outlet locks. You and Molly may come along."

Late in the afternoon, they arrived at Lock 13, or Deep Lock, which lowered vessels more than twelve feet. Watching the boat descend far into the lock, Josh looked over the stone wall and took a few steps back. "Careful," he thought. "If I fall in here, I'll be squashed between the boat and the lock wall. That might be the end of me!"

As they sailed under the railroad bridge, Josh was amazed to see how many factories and boatyards lined the waterway. And the canal was much wider here. There was room along the side for lots of boats to tie up and still be out of the way. The captain soon docked the boat at the Dugan Coal Company wharf. He hired workers to unload the coal under Mrs. Van Doren's supervision. Then the captain, Molly, and Josh walked along Burnet Street to the double outlet locks at the end of the canal.

Josh had never seen so many boats! Twenty or thirty vessels were lined up near the outlet locks, waiting to load or unload. Out in the Raritan River, just as many boats were waiting for a steam tug to tow them down the Raritan River toward New York City.

"When the canal first opened, " the captain told them, "there was only one lock at this end. But there's been so much traffic that the canal company built a second one alongside the first two years ago."

Suddenly Josh heard shouting and felt himself being pushed along by the crowd. Boatmen and onlookers alike were edging closer to the lock. What was going on? Josh squeezed between two husky deckhands and found himself staring at two boatmen who were slugging it out. "Why are they fighting?" he asked of no one in particular.

"Fighting over who goes through the lock next!" said a red-bearded captain standing on the lock wall. "Jacobus Van Arsdalen will put a stop to it right quick!"

Sure enough, the big, brawny locktender soon shoved his way through the crowd and, with the help of two sturdy boatmen, separated the brawlers. He made them pay a fine for delaying the other boats and then shouted to one of the captains to bring his boat in first. With the excitement over, the crowd dispersed.

Josh found Captain Van Doren and Molly talking with Mr. Van Arsdalen. The captain introduced Josh to the friendly locktender and continued his conversation.

Then, their business done, they all said their good-byes. The three canalers walked back along Burnet Street, stopping at Alderfer's General Store to buy a sweet treat for the children and some paisley curtain fabric his wife had been looking for.

Just before reaching the coal yard, the captain pointed out the Indian Queen Tavern, a popular stopping place for travelers who arrived by steamboat from New York City. Molly wanted to peek inside, but her father said that they must return to their boat to begin the trip home. "The Indian Queen can wait for another day."

By the time they reached Dugan's wharf, the coal had been unloaded and Mrs. Van Doren had supper ready in the cabin below. "Mr. Dugan says we may stay here until we're ready to leave," she explained. Josh climbed down the ladder and stepped into a tiny room filled with the mouth-watering smell of beef stew. He hadn't realized how hungry he was!

As the family gathered around the wooden table and said their prayers, he thought of his own family back home and blinked away a tear. Mrs. Van Doren gave him a hug. "You're always welcome at our table, Josh."

Knowing it would be light for another hour on this warm July night, Captain Van Doren decided to start back upstream. If they got through Deep Lock before nightfall, they could continue on and tie up for the night just below Lock 12.

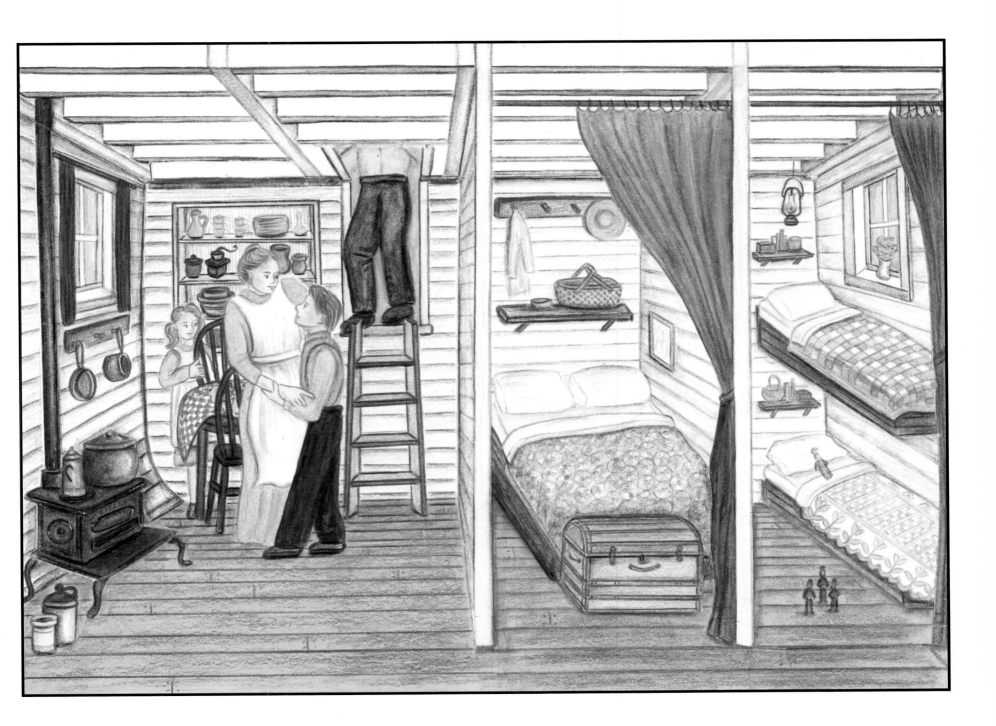

Before the sun came up the next morning, Josh awoke and wondered for a moment where he was. As the smell of oatmeal wafted through the cabin, he remembered.

The family was already up and moving. The captain was harnessing the mules, who had spent the night tethered to a tree. Mrs. Van Doren was preparing breakfast, and Molly was filling the mules' nosebags with oats. Josh finished his oatmeal and trotted down the plank onto the towpath as the captain fastened the towline to the harness. Then the lock gates opened, Daisy and Dorrie leaned forward, and the boat moved into the chamber.

Soon they stopped to pick up a load of hay and oats from Jacob Shurts, who sold grain and coal near the bridge in South Bound Brook. While waiting for the boat to be loaded, Mrs. Van Doren took Molly and Josh to Mr. Creed's grocery store.

"Let's see," she said, "we need meat, vegetables, candles, and tea. And, especially, a present for Sam."

They covered the next fifteen miles with no problems and arrived at the Griggstown bridge in mid-afternoon. After tying up below the bridge, they were amazed and happy to see Sam sitting on a bench outside the bridgetender's house. He was smiling and looking much better! Doc Wilson had said that Sam's leg was not broken, just bruised, and the lump on his head had gotten smaller.

Sam was thrilled to get a shiny, new baseball as a get-well gift from his mother. He wanted Sarah to toss it to him so he could practice catching.

Josh was happy to see his parents and his sister again. He had never been away from them for so long before. After a brief conference, the adults decided that Sam should stay off his leg for another couple of days. Josh would drive the mules to Trenton and back! This decided, Josh and the Van Dorens said good-bye to Sam and the Rileys and continued their trip.

Arriving at the Griggstown lock, Josh shouted "hello" to young Israel Reed. The Reeds had been locktenders here at Lock 9 for years. Israel was surprised to see Josh driving the mules. As they waited for the boat to ascend in the lock, Josh related the story about Sam's fall and his injured leg.

The *Atlantic* continued south next to the peaceful Millstone River. As they passed through the bridge at Rocky Hill, Josh saw a line of wagons delivering stone from the nearby quarry. He knew that canal boats, too, carried the rock from the quarry, because he had seen stone-filled vessels pass through his own swing bridge at Griggstown.

As they passed near the village of Kingston, Josh admired the tall, four-story mill next to the river. He wished he could explore the gears and machinery inside. It was much bigger than the mill at the Griggstown Causeway, near his own home.

About two miles past Kingston lock, they came to an amazing water-filled bridge — it carried the canal over top of the Millstone River! Soon after crossing this structure, the captain called to Josh to stop the mules. They would tie up here in Princeton for the night. During dinner, Captain Van Doren explained why the water-filled bridge was built.

"Sometimes," he said, "the canal has to cross a wide river. The men who built the canal knew that sometimes the river might be very low, and sometimes it might be in flood. Either way, it wouldn't be safe to take boats across. So, they built an aqueduct to carry the boats safely over top of the river."

In the morning, after another early start, the *Atlantic* tied up in the basin at Port Mercer to pick up supplies. "It's less crowded and noisy here than it will be in Trenton later on," the captain said.

By lunchtime they entered the outskirts of Trenton. A few minutes later the captain pointed out a stream of water coming into the canal. "That's the feeder, Josh. It brings the water from the Delaware River to fill the main canal."

The roar of factories and trains filled the air as they arrived at Coalport. Josh had never seen such a busy place! Trains of every description chugged by, pulling cars piled high with shiny, black coal. So many tracks that Josh could not count them! And every kind of boat — steam canalboats, tugboats, work scows, and mule-pulled boats like theirs.

And in the distance — "What are those buildings with the strange-shaped tops?" Josh shouted to the captain. "They look like upside-down funnels!"

"Those are the potteries that Trenton is famous for," answered the captain. "They make dishes, pots, bowls, roof tiles, sinks, and even fancy statues. And look yonder at the dome of our State House! That's where the lawmakers meet to make the laws for New Jersey."

"It's beautiful," Josh whispered.

At one dock, the *Atlantic* stopped to unload the hay and oats that were bound for Philadelphia on a larger vessel. Moving on downstream, they headed for the coal docks.

The captain waited his turn in line. Then, at a signal from the dockmaster, he poled his vessel alongside the railroad trestle of the coal company. In a moment, a stream of coal, like a river of black rocks, roared down from the railroad car above into the hold of the *Atlantic*. Captain Van Doren collected the bill of lading and signaled to Josh.

"Get up!" Josh called to the team. The mules didn't move. "Get up!" he shouted again, trying to be heard over the din of Coalport. Then Daisy and Dorrie twitched their ears and gently eased the vessel away from the coal docks, heading north to New Brunswick once again.

And so Josh happily spent the next week walking with the mules, enjoying the peacefulness of the river valleys and the noise and hubbub of the cities. Someday, he thought, I'll be the captain of my own canalboat, but for now, this'll do just fine.